Canada's Natural Resources

Carrie Gleason

Scholastic Canada Ltd.
Toronto New York London Auckland Sydney
Mexico City New Delhi Hong Kong Buenos Aires

Scholastic Canada Ltd.
604 King Street West, Toronto, Ontario M5V 1E1, Canada

Scholastic Inc.
557 Broadway, New York, NY 10012, USA

Scholastic Australia Pty Limited
PO Box 579, Gosford, NSW 2250, Australia

Scholastic New Zealand Limited
Private Bag 94407, Botany, Manukau 2163, New Zealand

Scholastic Children's Books
Euston House, 24 Eversholt Street, London NW1 1DB, UK

Library and Archives Canada Cataloguing in Publication
Gleason, Carrie, 1973-
Canada's natural resources / by Carrie Gleason.

(Canada close up)
ISBN 978-1-4431-0795-2

1. Natural resources--Canada--Juvenile literature.
I. Title. II. Series: Canada close up (Toronto, Ont.)

HC113.5.G54 2012   j333.70971   C2012-901651-9

6 5 4 3 2 1   Printed in Canada   119   12 13 14 15 16

Table of Contents

Rich in Resources

Natural resources are things found in nature that humans use. Sometimes the natural resources are necessary for our survival, like the water we drink, the food we eat and the materials we use to build shelter. Other natural resources are used to make our lives more comfortable. For example, video games and computers can make our lives more fun. Lots of different **raw materials** go into making electronic equipment, many of which come from **minerals** and **fossil fuels**.

Canada is a huge country, with oceans and rivers, forests and mountains, **fertile** soils and grasslands. Within all of these **environments**, people have found ways to use the natural resources that our land provides.

Let's see what Canada has to offer.

Chapter 1

Forests

From the stunted trees in the Far North to the forests of giant cedars on coastal British Columbia, over half of Canada is covered in forest. The most important natural resource in Canada's forests is its trees. Wood from trees is used in construction, papermaking and other **industries**.

There are eight forest regions in Canada. The types of trees, plants and animals that live and grow in a forest region depend on the climate and geography. About 180 tree species grow in Canada. Different types of trees mean a healthy forest that supports a variety of animals, insects and plants.

Canada's largest forest region is the Boreal forest, a "mixed forest," which stretches 5,000 kilometres across the country, from Yukon to Newfoundland.

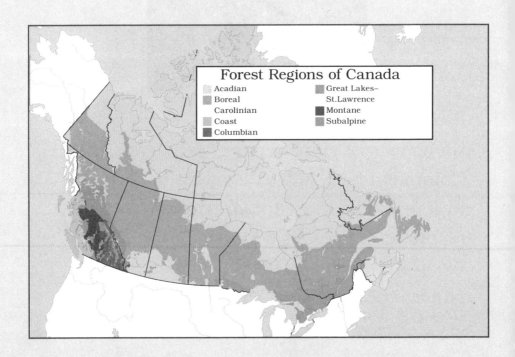

Forest Regions of Canada

Acadian
Boreal
Carolinian
Coast
Columbian

Great Lakes–
St.Lawrence
Montane
Subalpine

Mixed forest contains both **coniferous** and **deciduous** trees. It is also home to billions of birds, thousands of animals and hundreds of human communities.

The Great Lakes–St. Lawrence forest region is the second largest in Canada. It covers the southern parts of Ontario and Quebec, as well as southeast Manitoba. The trees here — including pine, birch, maple and oak — are similar to those in the forest region of the Atlantic provinces, called the Acadian region.

Canada's smallest forest region, the Carolinian forest in Ontario, is mostly deciduous trees. The other forest regions are in the West: the Coast region, the Columbian region, the Montane region and the Subalpine region of British Columbia and Alberta.

The terms "softwood" or "hardwood" are often used in the lumber industry. Softwood lumber comes from coniferous trees, such as pine, fir or cedar trees. Hardwood lumber comes from deciduous trees. Seeds from deciduous trees have a hard covering, like the acorns of an oak tree.

About one million hectares of forest is **harvested** in Canada each year. That is an area about twice the size of Prince Edward Island. This might sound like a lot, but one million hectares is less than one percent of Canada's total forest.

The business of cutting down trees is called the logging industry. People who work in this industry cut down trees, transport the logs, or do office and management jobs related to these activities. One of the decisions they make is what type of logging they want to do. They have three main choices: clear-cutting, selection cutting or shelterwood cutting.

In clear-cutting, whole sections of forests are cut at once, leaving behind large treeless patches. About 85 percent of logging in Canada is done by clear-cutting. Some people think this method is destructive because it harms forest habitats — the homes of the birds, insects and animals that live there. Others say it's better for the forest because it resembles a natural process, like a forest fire.

Clear-cut forest in British Columbia.

In selection cutting, only some of the trees are cut at a time, starting with those that are damaged or sick. This is more costly and time consuming for the logging companies, but better for the forest, since other forest plants and trees are left undisturbed. In shelterwood cutting, about a third of the trees are left standing, to drop their seeds and provide shelter for new trees to grow.

The industries related to forests provide jobs for about 600,000 Canadians.

Tree planters need to be dedicated and tough to go into remote areas to plant new trees.

After trees have been harvested from a forest, the logging company is responsible for making sure new trees are planted. Forests are renewable resources, which means they will grow back after they are harvested. But the rate at which they are used must be balanced with how fast they grow. This balance is called sustainability.

Why do we need living trees? Their leaves produce oxygen that we breathe, and absorb a harmful gas called carbon dioxide. Their roots can also help keep waterways clear by holding soil in place.

The logging company usually hires a company of tree planters to reforest where they have logged. Tree planters travel to the area where the trees were harvested. They often live in tents in the forest for several weeks or months during the planting season.

This may make it seem like there is an endless supply of forests, but any natural resource can run out if it isn't properly cared for. Caring for the forest also involves monitoring forest fires, plant diseases and insects that can cause harm.

Almost all (93 percent) of Canada's forests are publicly owned, which means the forests belong to all Canadians, rather than to individuals. The federal and provincial governments look after the forests for the people. Logging companies have to get permission from the government before they can go into a forest and start cutting. The companies also have to pay fees and provide a plan that shows how they will regrow the forest.

Canada is one of the world's biggest **exporters** of lumber and other wood products. Much of this is softwood lumber harvested from British Columbia's forests. Softwood lumber is used in the construction industry to build new homes. To make lumber, felled trees are taken to a sawmill to be cut into boards. Sawmills are usually located near forests and provide jobs for remote communities, especially in the provinces of British Columbia, Ontario and Quebec.

Softwood logs await processing in Quebec.

Forestry by province:

• British Columbia has Canada's biggest lumber industry. The province's most important trading partners are the United States, China and Japan.

• Saskatchewan is usually thought of as a prairie province, but over half of it is covered in trees! The forestry industry contributes about $1 billion a year to the province's economy.

• Wood-product manufacturing — making things like furniture, panels and cabinets — is Manitoba's most important forestry industry.

• The forestry industry provides hundreds of thousands of jobs in Ontario and Quebec.

• Pulp and papermaking are important industries in central and eastern Canada.

• The Christmas tree industry is especially important for the Atlantic provinces. Trees from the east coast are sent to central Canada and to the United States. Most Christmas trees are grown on tree farms.

Trees also provide the raw material for making different kinds of paper products, from books and newspapers to tissues and packaging materials. This is called the pulp and paper industry.

To make paper products, wood chips left over from the sawmill are sent to a pulp mill. There they are broken down into a soupy mixture (pulp) using either a chemical or a mechanical grinding process, depending on what the finished product will be. The Kraft process uses chemicals to make a pulp that results in strong paper products. Pulp for newsprint does not need to be as strong, so a combination of chemical and mechanical processes is used.

When the pulp is ready, it is sent to a paper mill to be made into paper. Quebec and Ontario both have large pulp and paper industries.

Newspapers printed on newsprint.

A papermaking machine in Quebec.

You care about the forests and want to make sure they're well cared for. But at the same time you like having copies of your favourite books and magazines to share with friends. What can you do? Look for the FSC symbol on forest products. FSC stands for Forest Stewardship Council. The FSC is an organization that works to make sure forests are well managed and that aboriginal peoples' rights to the land are respected. Companies that created the products, from the loggers to the manufacturers to the companies that sell the products to the stores, have all been investigated to make sure their practices are environmentally and socially friendly.

Living trees make healthy forests. Healthy forests allow other plants that we use to grow, like wild blueberries, mushrooms and fiddleheads. Canada is the world's largest exporter of wild blueberries. Some forest plants, like Canada yew or ground hemlock, are used to make medicines. Sap can be extracted from maple trees to make maple syrup. This industry is especially important to Quebec. In fact, Canada supplies 85 percent of the world's maple syrup.

Forests provide homes for animals, which are also natural resources. Animals can be hunted or trapped for their meat and furs. Animals, birds and insects help make sure the forests continue to grow by spreading seeds and **pollinating** new plants.

A swift fox curls up to stay warm in its natural forest habitat.

Taking care of natural resources is taking care of the environment.

Maybe best of all, healthy forests are places we can enjoy using. So the next time you go on a hike, a bike ride, a picnic or a camping trip in a forest, take a look around you and count the many ways the things you see can be used by humans.

Chapter 2

Oceans, Rivers and Lakes

Canada's motto is "from sea to sea." Not only is Canada surrounded by sea water on three sides, it also has one-fifth of the world's fresh water in its many rivers and lakes.

To the east of Canada lies the Atlantic Ocean, to the west is the Pacific Ocean, and to the north is the Arctic Ocean. Canada claims a 200-nautical-mile (370 kilometre) zone off its coasts, which is the area it calls its own fishing territory.

Water itself is an important natural resource. Fresh water is used for drinking and household activities like bathing and cooking. Water is also used in agriculture, **manufacturing**, mining and other industries. It is home to a variety of fish and plants, both in fresh water and in the salty oceans.

In some parts of the world, water is so rare and valuable that people fight over it. Canadians are fortunate not to have that worry. However, we have made mistakes managing our ocean resources in the past. Canadians have learned that we need to take better care of our water and its animals.

Fishing boats on the west coast.

Canada's fishing industry provides jobs for more than 94,000 people. In some places, whole communities depend on fishing for survival. The majority of what is caught (85 percent) is exported. Seafood is Canada's second-largest food export, after grain. The goods are shipped to 130 countries around the world, but mostly to the United States. This creates a $3.9 billion industry.

Canada has two million lakes and rivers. It has the largest fresh-water system in the world.

The first Europeans that arrived off Canada's coasts came for the fish of the Grand Banks. The Grand Banks is a 100-metre-deep underwater extension of the continent off the Newfoundland coast. Here, warm water from the Gulf Stream meets the cold water of the Labrador Current, creating the perfect environment for **plankton**, which is a big draw for the fish that eat them, especially cod.

For five hundred years, fishing boats came to the Grand Banks. By the 1950s, huge trawlers and factory ships were also working these waters, scooping up many tonnes of fish. But no one realized that cod were being removed from these waters faster than the fish could **reproduce**. By the 1990s, there were no more cod left.

For Newfoundland's fishing communities, the end of the cod fisheries meant they were out of a job. Many of these communities suffered when about 30,000 people were suddenly without work.

A crew lays out fish to dry in 1932. Dried, salted cod was the back-bone of Newfoundland and Labrador's economy until supply ran out.

In 1992, the Canadian government handed down a **moratorium** making it illegal to fish any more cod. Twenty years later, there is still no **commercial** cod fishery off Newfoundland. Will the cod population ever come back to what it once was? No one knows.

Because of what happened with the cod, Canada was one of the first countries to develop a code of conduct for its fishing industry in which they promise to take care of this resource.

Today the Atlantic provinces have a fishing industry that includes shellfish like lobster, shrimp and crab. Many of these fish are sold to other countries. Canada is the world's eighth-largest exporter of seafood.

Trawlers are ships that drag big nets behind them, scooping up all the ocean creatures in the water below. Factory ships are huge fishing ships that have refrigeration right on board. This means the catch won't rot if the ships stay out longer at sea to catch more fish.

Stacking crab pots on the docks at the end of a fishing season in St. John's, Newfoundland.

Crab, shrimp, clams and oysters are all important shellfish for the Canadian fishing industry, but the most valuable seafood export is lobster. Lobster is caught off the coast of Nova Scotia, the Bay of Fundy, the Gulf of Maine and the St. Lawrence. Most lobsters are caught in traps near the shore. To make sure there is enough lobster for the future, young lobsters and females with eggs are returned alive to the ocean if they are caught. The government gives out a limited number of lobster-fishing licences. The number of traps allowed is also closely monitored.

Lobster traps in Peggy's Cove, Nova Scotia.

British Columbia is Canada's top exporter of fish, followed by Nova Scotia, Newfoundland and Labrador, New Brunswick and Quebec. In British Columbia, salmon is the most valuable catch. Wild salmon are hatched from eggs in fresh-water rivers. The young fish then swim deep out into the Pacific Ocean. Once a year, adult salmon make their way back to the place where they were born to lay eggs. This event is called a salmon run. It is a huge journey for the fish and many don't make it. Commercial and sport fishers catch salmon during this annual **migration.**

Most of British Columbia's salmon catch does not come from the wild. To create a more stable salmon harvest, Atlantic salmon are raised on fish farms there. Atlantic salmon is not **native** to British Columbia and many people fear the effects the fish farms have on the environment. The fish are raised in pens along the coasts and in harbours.

Some people believe that the farms release diseases and **contaminants** into the ocean that will harm other marine life. Others fear that the pens will break and the Atlantic salmon will be released into the wild, where they will compete with wild salmon for their habitat.

Canada's fresh-water lakes and rivers also offer a supply of fish. In Lake Winnipeg, Manitoba, a large commercial fishing fleet catches Winnipeg goldeye, a small herring-like fish. Whitefish is caught in Alberta's northern lakes.

Grizzly bears like when the salmon run too!

Raising fish on farms is called aquaculture. It's one way to make sure the fish and shellfish we depend on today will be available for the future, rather than taking them from the wild. There are fish farms in every province and territory.

The oceans supply more than just fish. Irish moss is an algae, a type of water plant, that is harvested in Prince Edward Island. It is collected in shallow waters off the west coast of the province. Irish moss is used in beer, cosmetics and ice-cream making. It is Canada's most valuable seaweed crop.

Harvesting Irish moss in Prince Edward Island.

A fish farm in the Bay of Fundy, New Brunswick, where aquaculture has become an important industry.

Shellfish are raised on farms in Canada, including oysters, mussels, clams and scallops. Prince Edward Island produces the most shellfish in Canada this way. Farmed shellfish are available all year round. Eight species of fish are raised on fish farms in Canada, including salmon, trout and Arctic char. New Brunswick and British Columbia are the largest producers of salmon on fish farms. People are looking for ways to raise cod on fish farms, too. If they find a way, this could help restore depleted stocks in the Atlantic.

Chapter 3

Land and Soil

Canada is the second-largest country in the world. Of all of Canada's land area — 9,093,507 square kilometres — only a tiny portion (4.5 percent) is used for growing crops. Yet Canada is the world's fourth-largest exporter of **agriculture** products.

Healthy soil, water and the right climate are needed to grow food. Soil is made up of bits of rocks, sand, clay, water, air and **organic matter**. Tiny living organisms, like bacteria and fungi, are also found in soil.

All soil is not the same. In Prince Edward Island, for example, some of the soil is red. This is because the rock that the soil is made from has iron oxide, or rust, in it. In some areas of the Prairies, the soil is black. Often called "black earth," this soil contains a lot of organic matter. It is fertile soil, which means plants grow well in it. Areas of Canada that are covered in bare rock, like the mountains of the Rockies, can't grow crops because there is no soil.

The Canadian Soil Information Service has created a seven-class system to rank how well an area is suited to agriculture. Class 1 areas are the best for growing crops; class 7 areas cannot grow crops at all. More than half of Canada's class 1 farmland is in southern Ontario. But this is also the most populated part of the province, so the farms are competing with towns and cities for land.

Orchards and vineyards in the Okanagan Valley, British Columbia.

Because Canada has different regions and climates, some areas are better suited to agriculture than others. In the Far North, the ground is cold year-round and the summers are too short to grow many crops. In southern Ontario and Quebec, the growing season is longer. In some regions, like the Okanagan Valley and the Fraser Valley in British Columbia, the climate and soil are perfect for growing fruits and vegetables. In the Prairies, wheat and other cereal crops grow well.

Saskatchewan has
the most farmland
in Canada, followed
by Alberta, Manitoba
and Ontario.
About 12,000
years ago, parts
of Saskatchewan,
Manitoba and
Ontario were covered
by a giant inland
sea called
Lake Agassiz.
When the lake water

Prairie farms produce about
10 million tonnes of canola a year.

eventually drained away, it left behind the
rich farmland of southern Manitoba's Red
River Valley and Saskatchewan's fertile
Qu'Appelle Valley.

Saskatchewan's main crop today is wheat.
Wheat belongs to a group of crops called
cereal crops that also includes oats, barley
and rye, which are also grown in the
province. Saskatchewan supplies
10 percent of the world's wheat export.

Saskatchewan's second-biggest crop is canola. University scientists in Manitoba and Saskatchewan developed the canola plant about fifty years ago. The name comes from the words "Canadian" and "oil." Canola seeds are easy to grow in the prairie climate and when they are ground up, they provide a healthy type of cooking oil. Canola is also used in animal feed and **biofuel**.

Prairie farms and farms in Ontario and Quebec are known for growing animal feed. The types of crops grown to feed livestock include alfalfa, hay and corn. Farms in Alberta, Saskatchewan and Manitoba also grow sunflowers. Sunflower seeds are used to make birdseed.

The animal feed that is grown in Canada feeds the animals on livestock farms. Alberta produces 60 percent of Canada's beef cattle. Beef is the most important agricultural product in Alberta. Other farms across the country also raise dairy cattle, hogs and chickens. Some even raise bison.

Some of Canada's top agricultural products:

• Saskatchewan produces 99 percent of Canada's chickpeas. Chickpeas are part of a crop group called pulses, which includes peas, lentils and beans.

• The biggest potato producer in Canada is the province that's smallest in size — Prince Edward Island! Tiny PEI produces 26 percent of Canada's most important vegetable crop, potatoes.

• British Columbia farmers are involved in many activities, including dairy farming, growing apples, grapes and other fruits, and mushroom farming!

• The St. Lawrence River Valley is Quebec's most important agricultural area, for dairy farms and fruit and vegetable farms.

• Ontario's top agricultural activities are dairy farming and growing vegetables, soybeans and corn.

Like other industries based on natural resources, farming can take a toll on the environment. Soil is more delicate than it might seem. Good soil can be damaged by too much wind and water, or by drought.

Soil damage can be caused by poor farming techniques, overgrazing of livestock (too many animals grazing on the same patch of land) and pollution. Sustainable soil means farming in ways that put in as many **nutrients** as are taken out. Farmers do this by adding fertilizer to the soil and by rotating crops. Some farmers are switching to organic farming practices that don't harm the environment, such as using natural **pesticides** and fertilizers. Scientists also experiment to discover new plants that will grow better in certain climates.

An industrial irrigation system to water the crops in Saskatchewan.

Chapter 4

Rocks and Minerals

Some of Canada's most valuable resources —
its minerals — are nestled deep underground
in rock. Almost everything we use that does
not come from plants or animals is made of
some combination of minerals.

After three miners found gold in Bonanza Creek in 1896, nearly 40,000 prospectors flocked to the Yukon. Gold is a valuable mineral and everyone wanted to get rich! But very few people made their fortune from gold during the Klondike Gold Rush. Gold wasn't easy to find or extract. Dawson City, the town that sprang up when the gold rush began, shrank to a fraction of its population after it ended.

Today, gold is the top **metallic** mineral mined in Canada. Other important minerals are copper, nickel, zinc, iron and potash. Gold is used to make jewellery and in electronics parts. Huge mining companies bring in large machinery to build mines and processing facilities. But first, **geologists** have to find the minerals. They do this by drilling deep into the earth and removing rock samples to see if there are valuable minerals in the area. Gold and other minerals are usually found mixed together in a type of rock called ore.

An open-pit asbestos mine in Quebec.

To extract minerals from ore, the rocks are crushed and treated with water and chemicals. If mineral ores are found close to the surface, a method of mining called surface mining is done. Open-pit mining is a type of surface mining in which large holes or craters are dug into the earth to remove the ore. Another method of mining involves building an underground mine.

Canada's mining industry is one of the world's largest, with exports of more that sixty different minerals. The industry employs about 300,000 Canadians.

The types of minerals found in an area have to do with the geology of a place. The Canadian Shield is a broad, flat plate of the earth's **crust** that is more than 600 million years old. As well as having some of the oldest rock in the world, the Shield is also rich in minerals. Provinces and territories that lie on the Shield, like Manitoba, northern Ontario, northern Quebec, Labrador, the Northwest Territories and Nunavut, have strong mining industries.

When new mines are built in remote northern places like Nunavut, Inuit or Aboriginal people from nearby communities are trained and hired as employees. This helps provide employment in areas where there aren't many paying jobs. Once the mines have used up all the minerals, they will close. The employees will need to find other work. But now they will have job training and skills so they can find or create new jobs for themselves.

On the Quebec–Labrador border lies a deposit of iron ore that is 1600 kilometres long. Mining companies are planning to build more mines there. Iron ore is sold to other countries and to Canada's own steel industry. Steel is used to make skyscrapers, bridges, planes, cars and trucks, farm equipment and many other things.

Esterhazy, Saskatchewan, has the world's largest potash mine. Potash is a salt-like substance that is used to make fertilizer. Canada is the world's largest producer of potash.

The steel to make bridges and cars, the gold used to make circuits in electronics, the glass in windows and the pavement on roads — even toothpaste, sunscreen and cosmetics! — all come from minerals. No wonder people value minerals so much.

One of Canada's newest and most valuable mineral exports is diamonds. Diamonds and other mineral deposits were formed by natural processes over very long periods of time. For many years geologists believed there were diamonds hidden in the Arctic. After years of searching, they finally found them. Diamonds were discovered near Lac de Gras in the Northwest Territories in 1991. A diamond mine called Ekati was built. Several other diamond mines are now operating in the Far North, as well as the Victor Diamond Mine in Ontario. Canada now produces 8 percent of the world's diamonds.

Roads and railroads are built to move resources from where they are found to where they will be used. Railroads can't be built in the Arctic. And flying equipment in to build a mine, and then flying the diamonds out, is too costly. So the diamond mining companies join together to build a 600-kilometre "ice road" each year. The temporary road runs over a frozen body of water, to move goods to and from the mines' remote locations.

The ice road is only open from February until April, because that's when the ice is hard enough to support big trucks and keep their loads from falling into the icy Arctic water!

Here are some of the top minerals the
provinces produce:

- Ontario produces the most copper, gold,
nickel and silver.
- New Brunswick produces the most lead and zinc.
- Newfoundland and Labrador produces
the most iron ore.
- Northwest Territories produces the most diamonds.
- Alberta produces the most coal.

Sudbury, Ontario, is Canada's biggest mining town. Sudbury is located on the Canadian Shield. About 1.8 billion years ago, a meteor crashed into the Earth here. The meteor shattered into pieces, and the impact left behind a huge crater now called the Sudbury Basin. The force of the impact was so strong, it caused rock to melt. As the surface cooled, rich deposits of nickel and copper formed along the basin edges. These minerals were discovered there in the late 1800s when the railway was being built. When mining first began, copper was the most valuable mineral. As more uses for nickel were discovered, it too became valuable. Today nickel is used in stainless steel and batteries.

Unlike other resources, minerals are non-renewable. Once they are used up, they will be gone forever. When a

Sudbury's Big Nickel is a giant replica of a five cent coin.

mine runs out of minerals, towns can suffer because there will be many fewer jobs.

Mining also has an effect on the environment. Great amounts of water and chemicals are used to help separate minerals from ore. Afterwards, a substance called tailings is left. Tailings are toxic mixes of water and chemicals that are dumped back onto the land, where they pollute water in lakes and underground water supplies. Open-pit mines leave large physical scars on the earth, like huge craters.

One thing we can all do to help prevent some of the damage that mining causes to the environment is to be more aware of what we are buying. For instance, about sixty different types of minerals are needed to make a computer. When we create a higher demand for new computers, that creates an increased need for the minerals needed to make them, which affects the environment. We can all do our part by buying only what we need and by recycling.

Chapter 5

Energy Resources

Everything we do needs energy. Energy comes from a fuel source. Food is fuel for people. Sunlight and soil nutrients are plants' fuel. The most common fuels used today are fossil fuels — for transportation and to run factories, businesses and homes.

Coal, oil and natural gas are fossil fuels. They were formed from the remains of plants and animals that lived millions of years ago. When the plants and animals died, they were covered by mud and rock. As more mud and rock built up, the pressure and heat turned them into coal, oil or gas.

Coal is found in seams, or layers, underground. Strip mines are used to reach coal that is close to the surface. In strip mining, power shovels scrape away the layers of earth covering the coal. The coal is then collected for use. Underground mines are deep shafts dug into the earth, crisscrossed by tunnels that spread out into the coal seam. Miners use explosives and giant machines to drill out the coal, which is then sent to the surface.

Keeping miners safe is important in underground mining. Explosions and floods can happen, trapping miners underground. An explosion at the Westray Mine in Plymouth, Nova Scotia, in 1992 killed 26 miners.

A coal-fired power plant in Halifax, Nova Scotia.

Coal is a black or brown, rock-like substance that burns easily. In Canada, coal is mostly burned to make electricity in power plants and in factories that make steel. The rest is exported. British Columbia, Alberta and Saskatchewan have the most coal deposits. The largest coal mine in Canada is the Highvale strip mine, west of Edmonton, Alberta.

Natural gas is another fossil fuel. It is found trapped in **sedimentary rock** underground and beneath the ocean floors. Natural gas occurs by itself or with coal or oil. When natural gas is found with coal, it is called coalbed methane. Natural gas found in a kind of rock called shale is shale gas. To get the trapped gas, mining companies drill a well into the shale and pump in a mixture of water, chemicals and sand. This is called "fracking." It causes cracks in the rock, which frees the gas. The most natural gas drilling occurs in northeast British Columbia, in the Montney and Horn River shale basins.

There are big concerns about fossil fuels today. People worry about the pollution they cause when they burn. They also worry about what will happen when the supply of fossil fuels runs out. Some scientists have guessed that we will run out in the next one hundred years. Fossil fuels are non-renewable resources. It takes millions of years for new fossil fuels to form. Humans have used this natural resource much faster than it is being formed.

Natural gas pipeline laid out across Saskatchewan.

Natural gas is made up mostly of methane gas, but it also contains other gases and water. The other gases are removed during **processing**, before the natural gas can be used. Natural gas pipelines run across Canada and to the United States, delivering natural gas to where it will be used to produce electricity, or as fuel in homes and vehicles.

An oil well pumpjack in action.

Canada's main source of fossil fuels is the Western Canadian Sedimentary Basin, an area of sedimentary rock that lies under Alberta, southern Saskatchewan and northeastern British Columbia. Alberta has the largest fossil fuel **reserves**. Its first oil well was drilled at Leduc, just east of Edmonton, in 1947.

Oil and gas are drilled for under the seabed, too. This is called "offshore drilling." Hibernia, off the coast of Newfoundland, is the largest offshore oil platform ever built.

Today oil rigs still dot the countryside, but most of Alberta's oil is extracted from oil sands. At oil sands, oil is found mixed with sand. There are three separate oil sands deposits in the northern part of the province — in the Athabasca, Cold Lake and Peace River areas. The town of Fort McMurray is at the heart of the oil sands industry.

Oil is sent to a refinery and made into different products, especially gasoline for fuelling cars and trucks. Common household products are also made from oil, like plastics and certain types of cloth.

Oil sands in northern Alberta.

There are other sources of energy in Canada besides fossil fuels. Energy can also be transferred from one moving thing to another. The energy in moving water, for example, can be used to make electricity. Power that comes from moving water is called hydroelectricity. Canada is the world's largest producer of hydroelectricity.

The hydroelectric dam at Niagara Falls, Ontario.

Quebec has huge hydroelectric dams at James Bay and the Manicouagan River. In Ontario, a hydroelectric dam captures the energy of Niagara Falls. Manitoba, British Columbia and Newfoundland also have hydroelectric dams.

Saskatchewan is the country's top producer of uranium. Uranium, found in the mineral pitchblende, can be used to create electricity in nuclear power plants. Saskatchewan's McArthur River mine produces the highest-grade uranium in the world.

Uranium is radioactive. In nuclear power plants, uranium atoms are split and the energy this releases is used to create electricity. Nuclear power plants create huge amounts of energy, but they also create hazardous waste products that must be carefully stored.

All energy sources have an impact on nature. Mining fossil fuels can leave ugly scars on the landscape. Fossil fuels are also blamed for pollution and **climate change**. Hydroelectric dams divert the natural course of a river or flood areas of land.

Governments and companies in Canada spend time and money developing alternative sources of energy. Alternative energy is also sometimes called "green energy." It involves using biofuels, like fuel made from corn or canola, instead of fossil fuels. Wind and sun energy can also be captured and transferred into electricity. One of the world's largest solar-power farms is in Sarnia, Ontario. It can provide enough energy to power 300,000 homes. Wind farms across the country are producing enough electricity to power 1.5 million homes.

Pincher Creek, Alberta takes advantage of its status as the wind capital of Canada with this line of wind turbines.

What can we do to make sure there are energy sources and other natural resources for the future? A small step that can make a big difference is to be aware of the impact each one of us has on our natural resources. Start by asking questions to find out for yourself if the stuff you buy, the food you eat and energy you use is produced in a way that is sustainable for the future.

Glossary

agriculture: farming; agriculture products are crops and livestock that are raised on farms.

biofuel: a general term for the different types of fuel made from plants, trees or animal fat.

climate change: when long-term weather patterns are changed by human activity.

commercial: something done for profit, or to make money.

coniferous: trees with cones and needle-shaped leaves. Most stay green all year. Cedars, firs, larches, pines and spruce are coniferous trees.

contaminant: something that dirties or infects another thing.

crust: the rocky, outer layer of the Earth.

deciduous: trees that lose their leaves in the fall. Birches, maples, oaks, poplars and willows are deciduous trees.

environment: the physical surroundings of a thing, usually a plant or animal.

exporter: the seller of goods or services to another country.

fertile: the potential for reproduction, usually to create a new generation of plants or animals.

fossil fuels: substances burned for energy that were formed from the remains of ancient plants and animals. Coal, oil and natural gas are fossil fuels.

geologists: scientists who study geology, or the Earth and its rocks and formations.

harvest: the act of gathering a natural product in a season or year.

industries: business or economic activities, often grouped together by type of product made.

manufacturing: making goods for sale, usually by machines in factories.

metallic: how shiny something is. Minerals can be categorized by their lustre, or shininess.

Metallic minerals are shinier than non-metallic minerals.

migration: a seasonal move from place to place that some animals do for food or to reproduce.

minerals: naturally occurring, solid substances that are made up of chemical elements. Minerals are non-living.

moratorium: a legal suspension of an activity for a certain period of time.

native (to): being from a particular place.

nutrients: substances that are needed for health. Soil nutrients allow plants to grow and include chemicals like potassium and nitrogen.

organic matter: living things. In soil, organic matter usually refers to rotting leaves and other plant parts. It can also mean tiny living creatures and bugs in the soil.

pesticides: chemicals applied to plants to keep harmful insects, or pests, away.

plankton: tiny creatures that live in water. Plankton are the foundation of ocean food chains.

pollinating: the act of moving pollen from one plant to another. Pollen contains the material some plants need to reproduce, or grow new plants.

processing: to change something from its original state to a state in which it can be used or consumed.

raw materials: the starting material, usually natural, from which something is made. For example, a log is the raw material for a wooden chair.

reproduce: to create the next generation.

reserves: an amount of something set aside for future use.

sedimentary rock: rock formed from tiny bits or particles called sediment. Sedimentary rock forms in layers, or strata.

Index

Credits

Front cover: (trees) istockphoto.com/BrianGuest;
(fishing boat) istockphoto.com/mayo5;
(hydroelectric dam) istockphoto.com/IanChrisGraham.
Back cover: Tupungato/Shutterstock.com.

Page iv: gnohz/Shutterstock.com; p. 2: Elena Elisseeva/
Shutterstock.com; p. 3: Chrislofoto/Shutterstock.com; p. 4 (map art):
Paul Heersink; p. 7: Christopher Kolaczen/Shutterstock.com;
p. 8: Hugh Stimson; p. 10: Howard Sandler/Shutterstock.com;
p. 12: Lisa S./Shutterstock.com; p. 13: Moreno Soppelsa/
Shutterstock.com; p. 14: Matthew Jacques/Shutterstock.com;
p. 15: sianc/Shutterstock.com; p. 16: Bill Mack/Shutterstock.com;
p. 17: Brian Lasenby/Shutterstock.com; p. 19: Sebastien Burel/
Shutterstock.com; p. 21: The Rooms Provincial Archives Division,
VA 92-99/Attributed to Fred Coleman; p. 22: ejwhite/Shutterstock.
com; p. 23: Paul McKinnon/Shutterstock.com; p. 25: Tony Hunt/
Shutterstock.com; p. 26: Andre Jenny/GetStock.com; p. 27: Michele
and Tom Grimm/GetStock.com; p. 28: Melissa King/Shutterstock.com;
p. 29: Julija Sapic/Shutterstock.com; p. 31: Lijuan Guo/
Shutterstock.com; p. 32: Bryan Sikora/Shutterstock.com;
p. 35: Elena Elisseeva/Shutterstock.com; p. 36: Paul Binet/
Shutterstock.com; p. 37: Terry Davis/Shutterstock.com;
p. 39: meunierd/Shutterstock.com; p. 43: courtesy of Diavik Diamond
Mines Inc.; p. 44: Mark52/Shutterstock.com; p. 46: Bruce Raynor/
Shutterstock.com; p. 47: Steve Cukrov/Shutterstock.com;
p. 49: V. J. Matthew/Shutterstock.com; p. 51: Pictureguy/
Shutterstock.com; p. 52: Brenda Carson/Shutterstock.com;
p. 53: Christopher Kolaczan/Shutterstock.com; p. 54: martellostudio/
Shutterstock.com; p. 57: 2009fotofriends/Shutterstock.com.

The Son replies, "The only thing that would keep us from our obligation of honoring this hope is if Larry Smith and the others give up this hope."

We must not give up such a strong hope as this!

Our hope is only as strong as that which we hope in or have gotten our hope from. If it comes from God and is placed in God, it is as sure as heaven itself. This kind of hope won't keep us from the disasters of life, but it will keep us through them.

"Hope is there to hold us up when everyone else and everything else lets us down."

If we can just get enough courage to cry out to God in the time of our struggle, then we know with great assurance that God is there and hears us. We may not understand His timing or His response, but we don't have to. We do know that He has our best interests at heart.

Trials are not easy. No one would ask for them, but trials need not throw us into despair. Grasp hold of hope in those tough times. Hope is there to hold us up when everyone else and everything else let us down.

Remember, no one can take our hope away, not even Satan himself. He can only deceive and throw up those obstacles that God allows. The larger the obstacle, the more we know how much God is sure we are able to bear and conquer the trial.

A simple Chinese proverb says, "In no prairie fire do seeds perish; see, their new blades shoot forth amidst the spring breezes." Let everything turn to black ashes, but as long as there is the smallest seed of possibility, there is hope. The way to keep a strong hope is to have everything tested, right down to your determination to hold on and not give up.

It is the hard times that prove the strength of what we truly believe. Hope keeps us holding on for the recovery, the new day, the next breath of fresh air. Hope is not so hard to grasp and hold onto. Grab hold and don't let loose!

Hope cannot be forced on us. Hope can only be accepted or surrendered. The only person who can undermine your hope is you. Don't give up hope. Why surrender something as sure as our hope in God?

If we can hope, even in the hardest of times, we can take heart because faith is close behind.

Page

59   "Victor Frankl is known for his writings…"
       Victor Emil Frankl, *Man's Search for Meaning*
       (Boston: Beacon Press, 1962), 104.

59   "Chuck Swindoll calls attention to…"
       Charles R. Swindoll, *Dropping Your Guard*
       (Waco, Tex.: Word Books, 1983), 193.

59   "Frankl helps us see this idea…" *Search*, 74.

60   "Frankl attributes the ultimate cause…" *Search*, 74-76.

85   "Theodore Roosevelt said…"
       Theodore Roosevelt, speech given to the Hamilton
       Club, 10 April 1899, Chicago.

86   "Charles Brower said…"
       Charles E. Jones, *Life Is Tremendous*
       (Wheaton, Ill.: Tyndale House Publishers, 1969), 15.

87   "This was Abraham Lincoln's response…"
       Dale Carnegie, *How to Enjoy Life and Your Job*
       (New York: Simon & Schuster, 1985), 60.

106   Judson Cornwall points out…"
       Cornwall: *Unfeigned Faith*, 44.